Tiny Miracles

Sheryl Tirol

Presentation by *BookLeaf Publishing*

Web: www.bookleafpub.com

E-mail: info@bookleafpub.com

ISBN: 9789357440264

First edition 2023

DEDICATION

To Mom & Dad

For always having faith in my creative spirit

ACKNOWLEDGEMENT

I haven't written a poem in years and this last
year I got some unexpected inspiration from a
writing instructor who assigned us to write one in
class and off I went! I have plenty of folks to
thank but first, my thank you to God for helping
me realize where my gifts and talents are and my
love for writing.

I also want to thank my family, Brian, Brad,
Anna and Luke Tirol for always listening to all of
my ideas. I also extend my gratitude to my LA
family, the Gupilan clan - Uncle Carlo, Aunt
Dawn (Jing), Krystle, Kris, Kinzie, Kevin, Kiara,
and Pumba of course! You have all been an
incredible support to me over the years.

To my friends, Barb Watkins, Christina Martin,
Carmen Hagevoort, Natalie Alvarez, Mike and
Traci Grimm, Kevin Nazal and all of my St.
Monica pals for your friendship and love. To
Katie Breaux who like me is a complete book
nerd and always encouraged my writing.

To my forever Cornerstone Sisters for always
praying for and encouraging me - Lauren,

Donna-Mae, Elizabeth, Preethi, Sarah and Steph
-- I love you gals!

Thank you to my colleagues at Regis University
for always helping me and being an incredible
support system.

To my parents, Rey and Diana Tirol for always
believing in my creative spirit which was at times
a challenge - thank you for always believing in
me and finally to my grandparents Doris and
Prudencio St. Lucia and Rosario and Rupert de
Castro who are no longer here with us but who
have always and continued to inspire me.

PREFACE

Each day brings us a new season and in this collection of poems we get a glimpse into how our faith and love for the simplicity of this life can bring each of us tiny miracles.

Mary Undoer of Knots

She stands above the sun and stars
She is clothed in blue
Twelve stars appear before her head
She is a ray of light…
She holds a thick ribbon where the bottom has a
few knots…
but are unfurling…
The knots are coming undone slowly…
I look to her to intercede for me…
To help undo the knots in my life…
To help guide me
She has a face of beauty…
A face of purity and love…
Yet there is so much strength in that angelic face
She holds a place in heaven with the angels…
With the saints…
With our loved ones….
She watches over us
And when you ask for an intercession…
A plea for help…
It does not go unanswered …
It is never too late
And not on my time but when needed
For she is the Mother of God…
He knows what is best for us…
And his Mother will always gently guide us

So I look to her now in awe…
In inspiration…
With my heart full of love
There are no guarantees these knots will come
undone tomorrow but they will eventually…
For I know that she always intercedes
She always comes to my aid…
Oh Mary Undoer of Knots
Pray for us
For we know your love is like no other

December 21st

3

December 21st - the darkest and shortest day of
the winter solstice
A reminder that while it is cold and dark…
Light is soon returning
Winter brings us darkness but also rest,
Comfort and peace
With each day passing a new season is
approaching
So embrace today the darkest and shortest day….
For soon the sun and spring will arrive

He Always Restores

When it seems the pain is endless
That this hole you have dropped into has no end
to it
A gentle reminder that there is light near you…
That darkness will soon move on
A gentle reminder that not all hope has been lost
That peace will soon arrive
A much-needed respite is on the horizon
So while it seems there is no end to this…
Remember God is closer than you think…
He hears those pleas and is quietly working
through it all

Why

She wanted desperately to find out why
But no reason would suffice
But she prayed, plead and searched far and wide for a
why
Those prayers and pleas were not answered the way
she thought they would
It was in time
Day by day
Morning and night
She let go…
And began to live again
She started to see why the rising of the sun mattered…
And why the sun setting and seeing the moon lit was a
gift
Life will never move in a straight line
There will always be peaks and valleys along the way
But this life is one to treasure
Despite not getting the reason "why"…
She realized it is in giving her heartaches to the
universe…
And keeping her heart open that the reason no longer
mattered
She just kept moving forward embracing what might
come her way

Grief

Silence sweeps through the still air
Nothing can be heard...
It's as if the world is standing still for a moment
But life goes on and moves forward
Only memories can be remembered and felt
A stolen kiss...
A boisterous laugh...
A warm touch...
Now a distant memory
But while grief is painful...
It is a reminder to those still living to never take
this life for granted
For people and their love are what keep us alive
in this life now
It is with open hearts
That those we lost
Will never be forgotten
For grief can be a gift despite the hurt that
we always must do better

London

Oh London how I love thee

The feel of history upon my feet

Hyde Park and Notting Hill…

Buckingham Palace and the Pancreas…

The London Eye, The Savoy and even Harrods…

Tower of London which holds those Crown Jewels…

Oh London how I love thee

English tea near the Thames…

St. Paul's Cathedral and Westminster Abbey…

Kensington and St. James all palaces fit for royals…

Oh London how I love thee

Piccadilly Circus and Trafalgar Square…

Big Ben…so much more…

Oh London how I always love thee

Time

Time is always going
It never stops
Even when we want to...
The clock remains to keep us going
But in those slow moments when we pause...
It sometimes feels as though time has also stopped
We can feel the air...
We smell and taste much more
We see clearer...
But alas time is still going
It is up to us to make the most of the time we have
For before long...
Time will continue
But we will be long gone

The End

How does one honor the end of something?
The end of a chapter
a moment
an experience
a relationship
or
even a person
One must close the chapter with a grateful heart
Like death
It must be closed with a prayer of thank you
Some endings are painful
And one must mourn it...
But you can always receive it as a gift
A way to let go
To give way for something new
A new beginning and a fresh start
To honor the memory and reflect
While keeping one's heart open full of love
To be able to go forward and only look back once
Only to say goodbye
And look ahead for something even greater than what
was once before

Heart

I feel my heart can be moved in different ways
It can be aching like a tiny puncture wound...
Or leaping for joy filled with hope
But the heart needs to be guarded while remaining open
You can give the heart over to anyone
It must be protected while allowing you to still love...
It is a balancing act to have a heart of love
It cannot be closed off but needs to be tendered with care
Yes the heart can get carried away...
And can be hurt...
But the heart is much bigger than we give it credit for...
It can also love through the pain
And can be the gentle touch one needs to give to someone
else
Never take the heart for granted
For it will always be there and you must always find a way
To love through it all

Friendship

Friendship is a precious gift
A chance to connect and a way to nurture one's heart
While certain friendships come and go...
It is the meaningful ones we hang onto
The friend who goes the extra mile to help mend a broken
heart...
Make us laugh for no reason
Give us comfort in times of grief
To be adventurous with us when we can't do it alone
To be our cheerleader when life becomes too difficult
To help keep us accountable when we go astray
Yes friendship is a gift
And it is in how we give and receive that keeps it going
strong

Sisters

The one we call when we are in despair…
Who answers without judgment and only with care
When it seems we cannot see the light…
You never give up on me and help me understand I must continue to fight
Who helps me see what my true gifts and dreams are…
Even if it seems far
She will always be up for that adventure to see a different place…
And will always be there to give you that needed embrace
A loving and kind voice…
Years later still here by choice

Winter

Cold, grey, dark

It can feel empty…

But warmth can be felt in this season

Cozy and comfy

Days spent inside

Drinking hot tea or warm cider

Curl up near a fire with a blanket and a good book

A time to go inside…

To rest and honor this time for me

For snow and the iciness of winter

Will end soon…

And a new season that is warmer and vibrant…

Will bring us back outside…

To bring us near our friends once again

Giving It Back to God

She knew the time came

She could no longer hang on…

For she had already given her heart away…

But had been left with disappointment

She prayed and asked for clarity…

For wisdom…

For peace…

In the end she heard that voice

Calling to her once again

It was but a faint sound…

A whisper…

Saying…

It is time to give this back to me

To let go

To allow the burden to be released

To acknowledge

She did all she could…

Tried and then tried again…

And tried even harder

But alas it was no longer hers…

No more tears and heartache

But respite

As she realized the prayer was being answered

In giving it all back to God

For He would carry the load now…

And allow her to rest…

And to heal her heart

The Strangers

For they come far and near

Some from planes, trains, boats and even foot

They are strangers…

Foreign to this land

They come up with family, friends and others like them

Seeking a new dream…

Not one of wealth and honor

But for prosperity…

A simple wish

One that keeps them safe

Gives them a chance

To be able to contribute

To do good

To provide for their loved ones

They hope that while there are those who do not welcome them…

Others will embrace them and give them opportunity

For this life is short…

We know not where we will one day end up after our time is
finished here on earth

So to the stranger who comes wanting a chance

For a roof under their head

A warm bed and a meal…

The chance for human dignity

May God give you that courage as you journey to this land

May we find compassion in our hearts

For we too once had ancestors journey who were not
welcome

Who had to make their way

For us to enjoy the comfort of this life we now have

St. Raphael

You are the archangel who led two lovers to one another

The blessed saint whose name means healing

The one that believed that good will win over evil

Oh St. Raphael may you watch over me on this journey of life…

May your help lead me to the one I am meant to be with…

To help me see our own power to also heal others…

With love, kindness and compassion

For you archangel are the one who blessed those who came to feel and see your presence…

May we all be able to one day also feel that light and love

Best Friend

Best friend, how is it this much time has come and gone

Best friend, how has life quickly sped up and now…

We are living different lives in homes not near one another

Best friend, If ever I depart this earth before you…

May you know how very much I love and care about you

How your friendship has been an infinite gift

One that has not only healed but grown in love

And if ever we cross paths again best friend…

May you always carry with you this knowledge of my gratitude to you…

That you will always be cherished…

And that you will have a special place in my heart for you

Journey

The trip may be long

But it will always be worth it

Along the way…

There will be bandits and thieves who want to rob your heart and soul

But there will also be angels and saints who will help and love you…

Who want the best for you

The trip is filled with perilous dangers…

But there are also many beautiful places to see…

Oceans, valleys, mountains, sunrises and sunsets…

And plenty more to see and feel

Never stop even if you fall and you will stumble many, many, many times…

But get up…even if it is painful and hard…

Even if you move slower than before…

Keep going…

For there is plenty left to see and experience

For this journey we call life will be ever
expansive

And one worth fighting for

New Beginnings

Can you feel it?

A new chapter is unfolding…

An updated timeline…

With a new setting and new characters

A fresh slate yet to be tackled…

A new opportunity that feels scary but also
exciting

For new beginnings are just that

A chance to begin again…

To seek something better and to give you a
chance to grow

New beginnings will stretch us…

For the ending of the last chapter may have
broken us…

But we did not stay broken forever…

The pain subsides a bit…

And we keep moving forward

For new beginnings are just that

A way to awaken us

To make us realize

We cannot remain stagnant in this life

We must continue growing and getting stronger
along the way

To give us the gift of wisdom

To take a chance when we are not sure

For new beginnings are just that

A new chapter to hope once again

Parents

They are the ones who create your life…

A mother who carried you in the womb and brought you into the world…

A father who sheltered, loved and protected you…

The two people who will scold you when you have done wrong…

But champion you in the end…

Who will love you unconditionally on your good and bad days…

The two people who decided before you came they loved and wanted you…

For parents have the toughest job in the world…

To help a tiny human become a full-fledged person who will go into the world…

To hopefully fulfill their dreams

For parents we thank you for not giving up on us…

And always loving us

Brothers

Brothers are the gift of partners one has

Whether they are older or younger

Their call is to protect you

Your first partners in life

Brothers who are the ones who will relentlessly tease
and aggravate you…

But who will hold you near when everything falls
apart

Brothers who help you when you are in trouble…

But will celebrate you with your wins in life

For brothers are for life…

They are the only ones we can call in the middle of the
night or early at dawn…

Brothers who in the end are tied to you not just by
DNA…

But by heart

God

He met me one night

It was late and I was tired…

Exhausted and hopeless…

Scared and anxious about what was next…

He embraced me

Took me in his arms…

Led me by hand to a place of peace and comfort

He met me on a day when I was in tears and heartbroken…

I knelt in prayer unsure of what to do…

He lifted my chin and held me close…

He comforted my heart and while the pain did not completely go away…he eased it

He met me one morning when the whole world stopped…

When it wasn't even possible to see those who I love and

care about…

When everything seems to turn upside down and go
into
chaos…

My mind and heart was restless…

He met me that afternoon on the beach…

While I contemplated where my life was heading

He met me on the top of the mountain…

And near the valley and lake where the sun was
shining
bright…

And I came to know him on the drive over the
mountain tops
during one sunrise…

He met me the day I decided it was time to move
forward…

God never gave up even when I wasn't sure what was
to
happen…

He believed in me so I would have the courage and
strength
to keep going